READING/WRITING COMPANION

Cover: Nathan Love, Erwin Madrid

mheducation.com/prek-12

Send all inquiries to:
McGraw-Hill Education
Two Penn Plaza
New York, NY 10121

ISBN: 978-0-07-901787-1
MHID: 0-07-901787-8

Printed in the United States of America.

6 7 8 9 LMN 23 22 21 D

Welcome to Wonders!

Explore exciting Literature, Science, and Social Studies texts!

- ★ READ about the world around you!
- ★ THINK, SPEAK, and WRITE about genres!
- ★ COLLABORATE in discussions and inquiry!
- ★ EXPRESS yourself!

my.mheducation.com

Use your student login to read texts and practice phonics, spelling, grammar, and more!

(t) George Hall/Code Red 2012; (c) Paul Souders/Photodisc/Getty Images; (bl) Rob Marmion/Shutterstock; (bc) Thomas M Perkins/Shutterstock; (br) vipman/Shutterstock

Unit 4 Around the Neighborhood

The Big Idea

Week 1 • Time for Work

ML Harris/Iconica/Getty Images

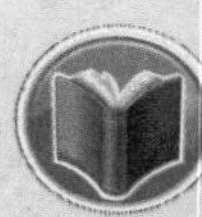

Digital Tools *Find this eBook and other resources at:* my.mheducation.com

Week 2 • Meet Your Neighbors

Week 3 • Pitch In

Writing and Grammar

Wrap Up Units 3 and 4

Unit 4

Around the Neighborhood

The Big Idea

What do you know about the people and places in your neighborhood?

Talk about what the neighbors in the picture are doing.

Circle the neighbors who are playing together.

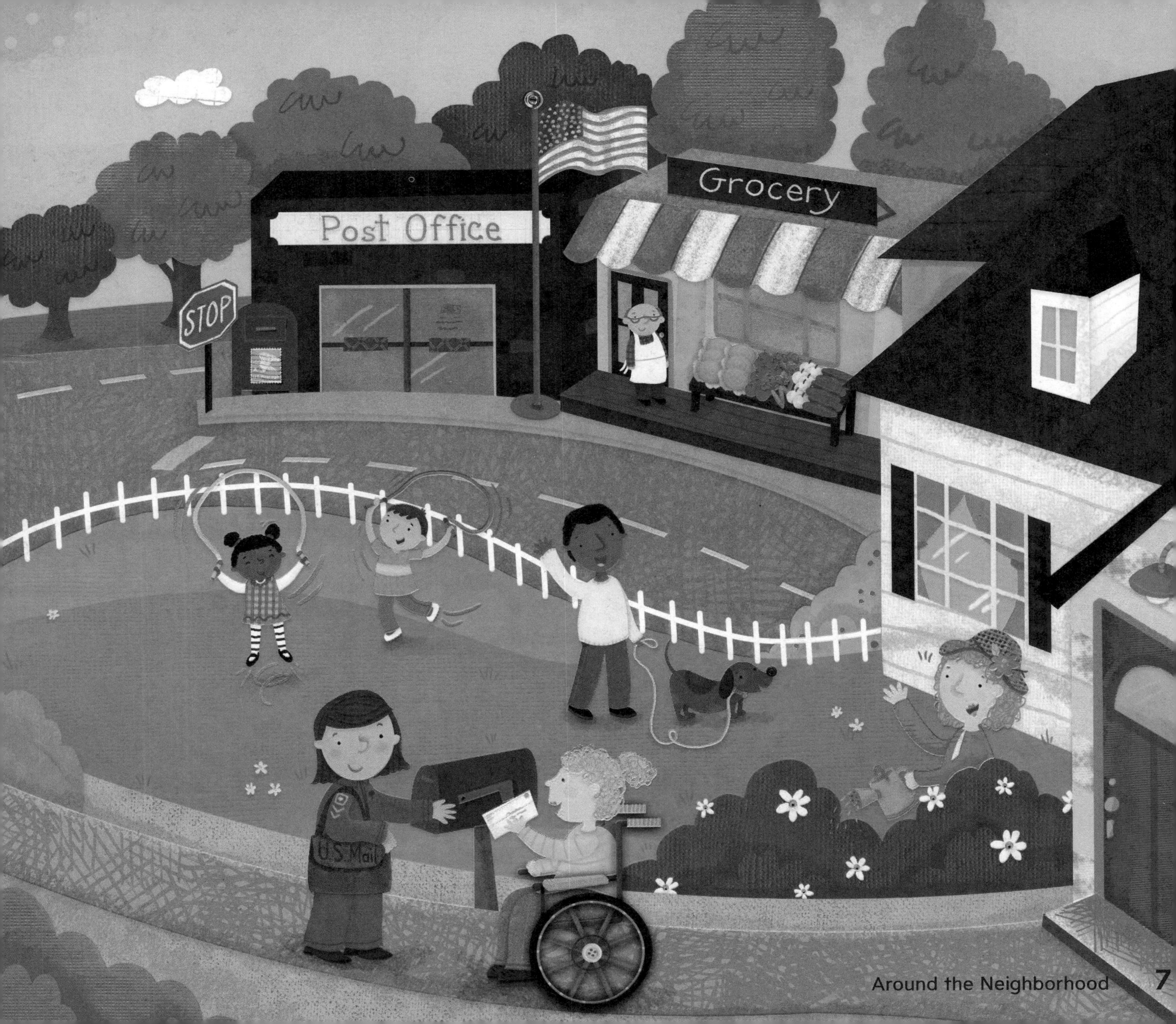
Grocery
Post Office
STOP
U.S. Mail

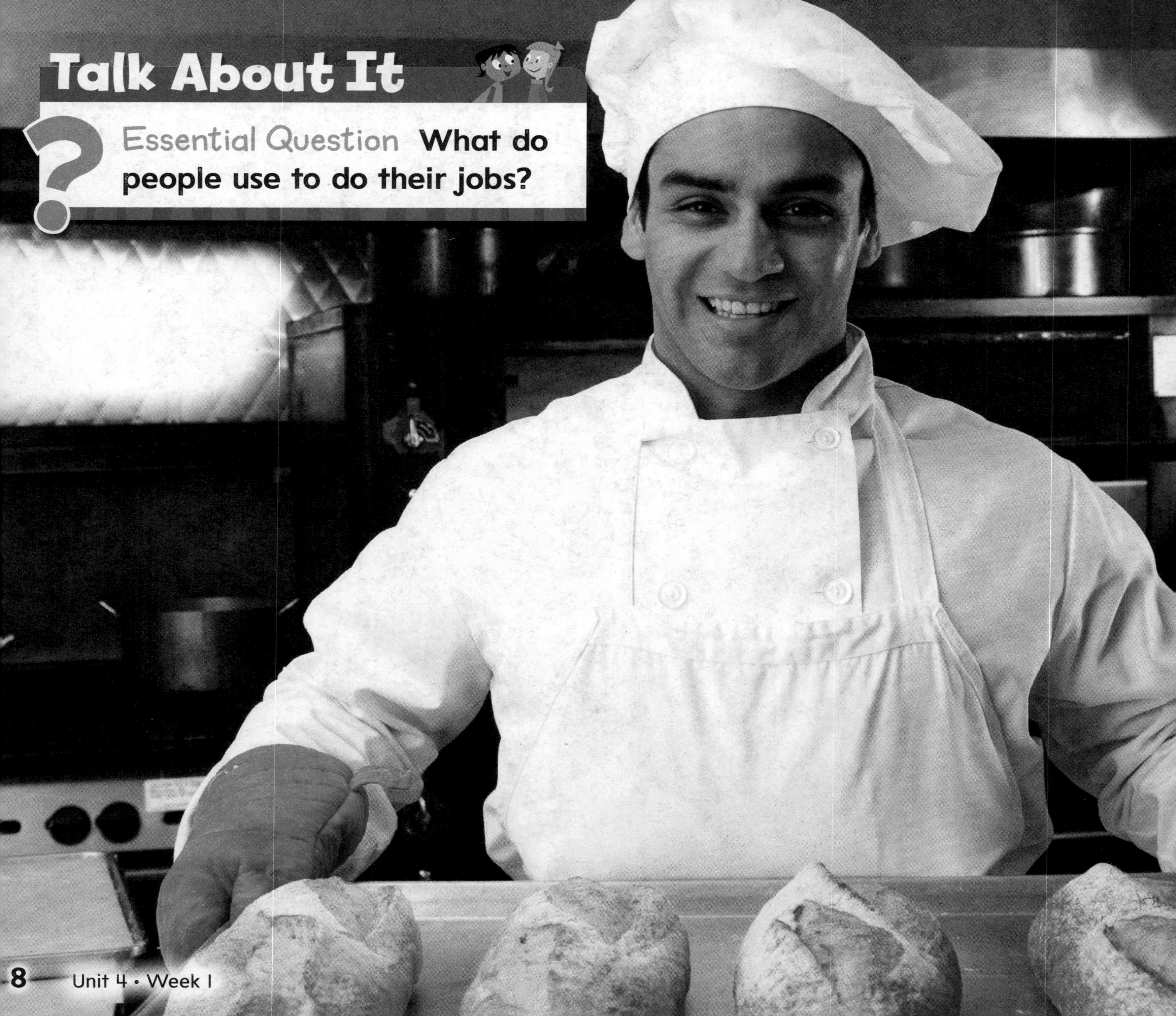

Talk About It

Essential Question **What do people use to do their jobs?**

 **Talk** about the tools this cook uses.

 **Draw** and **write** about another tool a cook uses.

A cook uses

Read

Respond to the Big Book

 **Retell** the nonfiction text.

 **Write** about the text.

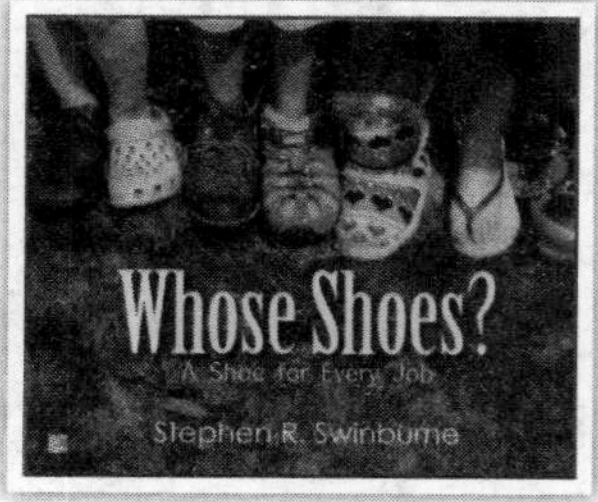

An important fact I learned is

Text Evidence
Page

An interesting part of the text is

Text Evidence
Page

Talk about special clothing that workers wear.

Draw and **write** about a worker who wears special clothes.

This worker wears

Reread **Big Book**

Key details in the words and photos in a nonfiction text give important information about a topic.

 **Listen** to part of the text.

 **Talk** about the key details.

 **Write** two key details.

Two key details are

1. ______________________________

2. ______________________________

 **Draw** one key detail you wrote about.

 **Talk** about how the words and photos help you learn the information.

Big Book

Listen to pages 13–18.

Talk about how each question has an answer.

Draw the answer to the question on page 13.

 **Look** at pages 25–30.

 **Talk** about how the author shows that each shoe goes with a worker.

 **Draw** and **write** about a shoe from the text.

This shoe is good because

Shared Read

Tom On Top!

 **Find Text Evidence**

 Read to find out about a firehouse.

 Circle the word **you.**

(bkgd)Susan Kuklin/Photo Researchers/Getty Images; (t)Jenna Riggs

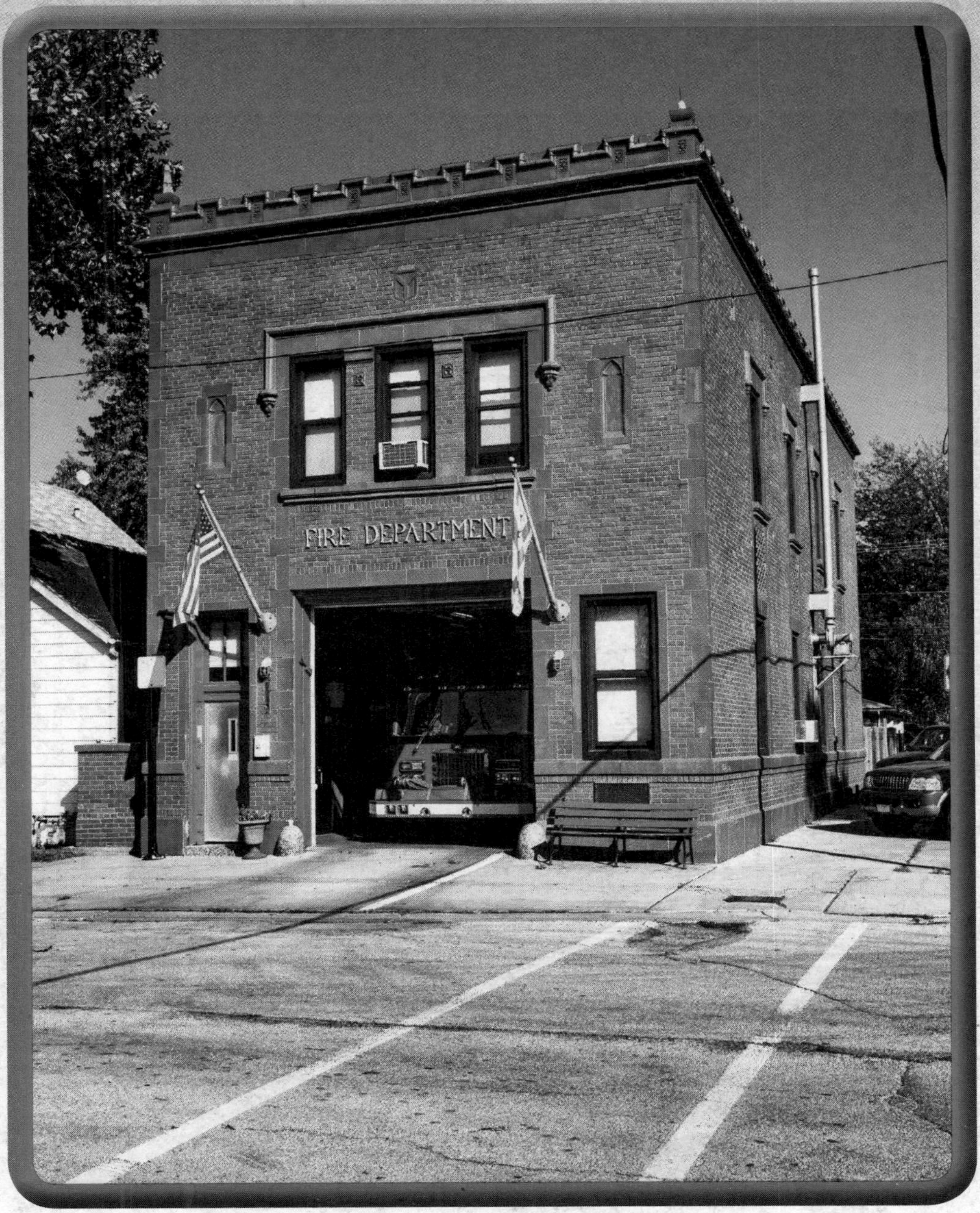

Can you see a ?
firehouse

(t)stevegeer/iStock/Getty Images; (b)Jenna Riggs

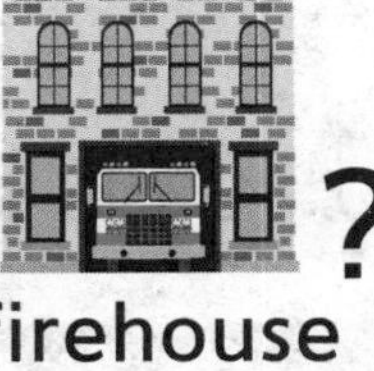

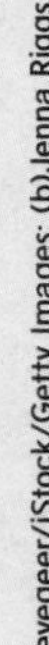

Shared Read

Find Text Evidence

Ask questions you may have about the text as you read. This can help you learn information.

Read each sentence. Point to the first letter and end mark in each sentence.

I can see a fire truck.

(l) Richard Semik/Alamy; (b) Jenna Riggs

I can see a firefighter.

Shared Read

Find Text Evidence

Circle what is red on page 20.

Underline the lowercase letters on page 2I.

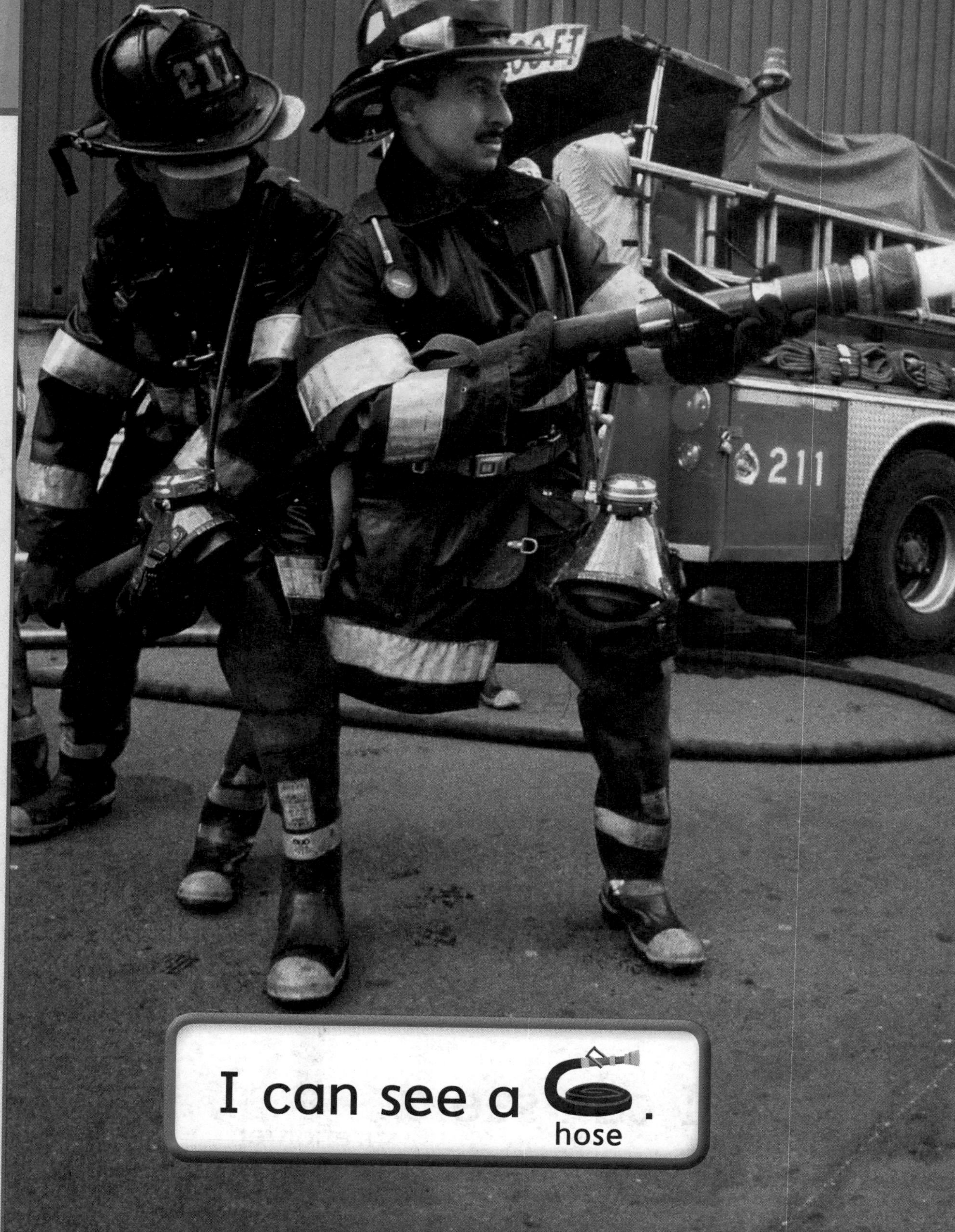

I can see a hose.

I can see a  hat .

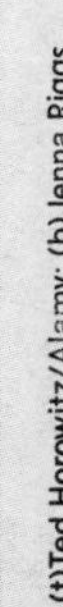

Find Text Evidence

Circle words that have the same middle sound as **mop**.

Retell the text. Use the words and photos to help you.

Richard Hutchings/Photo Researchers/Getty Images

I can see a pot.

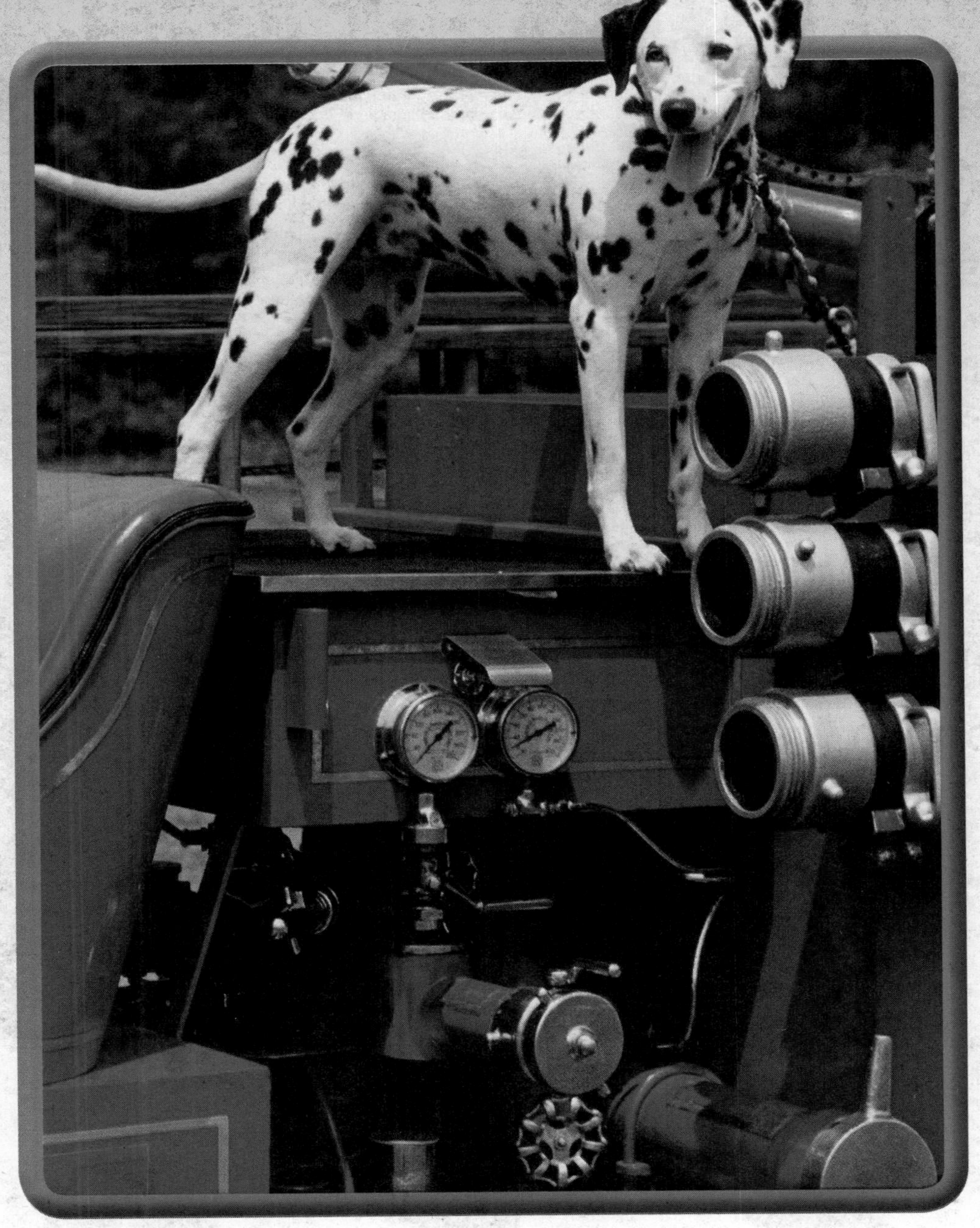

I can see Tom on top!

George Hall/Code Red 2012

Reread **Paired Selection**

Look at the photos. What tools do firefighters use?

Talk about the tools you see in the big and little photos.

Draw a line from the tool in the little photo to the same tool in the big photo.

Quick Tip

You can use these sentence starters:

Firefighters ______.
They use ______.

hose

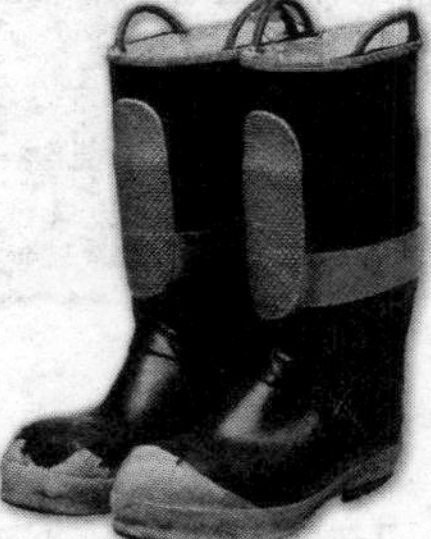

boots

helmet

Talk about the tools in the little photos. Choose one to write about.

Write how this tool helps firefighters.

This tool is

This tool helps firefighters

Talk About It

What can you learn from the big and little photos? What do the labels tell you? Why does the author include photos and labels?

Workers and Their Tools

Step 1 **Talk** about jobs and the tools workers use. Choose a job.

Step 2 **Write** a question about the tools the worker needs to do that job.

Step 3 **Look** at books or use the Internet. Or talk with a worker who does that job.

Step 4 Draw and write about what you learned.

Step 5 Choose a good way to present your work.

Make Connections

Talk about what this worker is doing. What tools is he using?

Compare these tools to the tools you read about in other texts this week.

Quick Tip

We can take a close look at photos to learn information.

What I Know Now

Think about the texts you read this week.

The texts tell about

Think about what you learned this week.
What else would you like to learn?
Talk about your ideas.

Share one thing you learned about nonfiction texts.

Talk About It

Essential Question **Who are your neighbors?**

Talk about how these people are being good neighbors.

Draw and **write** about one way you can be a good neighbor.

I can be a good neighbor by

Respond to the Big Book

Retell the realistic fiction story.

Write about the story.

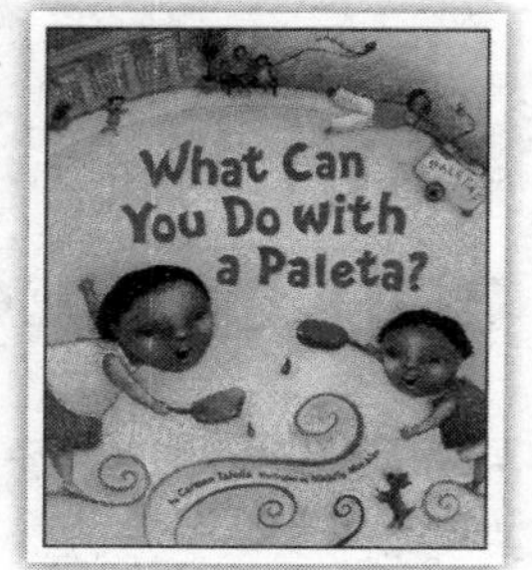

A paleta is good because

Text Evidence

Page

This is realistic fiction because

Text Evidence

Page

Talk about what the neighbors do with a paleta.

Draw and **write** about what you would do with a paleta.

I would

Make Inferences

Why is it a special event when the paleta wagon comes? How is a paleta more than just something to eat?

Reread **Big Book**

Characters are the people or animals in a story. The setting is where the story takes place. The events are what happen.

Listen to part of the story.

Talk about the characters and the setting.

Write about the characters.

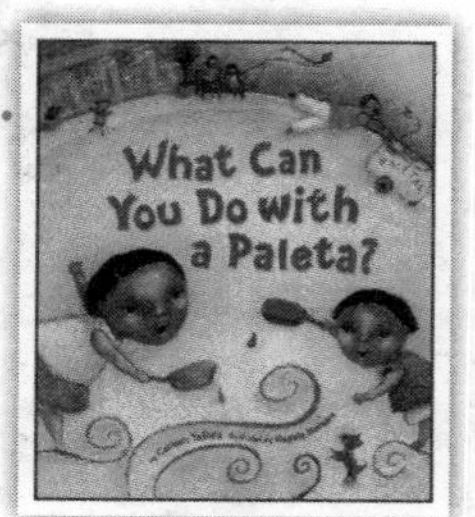

The characters are

____

____

____

Draw and write about the setting.

The neighborhood has

Reread **Big Book**

Listen to page 27.

Talk about how the girl's words help you to see, feel, and smell the roses.

Draw and **write** about the roses. Use words from the story to help you.

The roses are

Listen to pages 26–31.

Draw and **write** about the character who is telling the story. What might she say about her barrio?

Quick Tip

You can use other words in a story to help you know what a word means. Listen as your teacher rereads part of the story. What do you think **barrio** means? How do you know? Tell your partner.

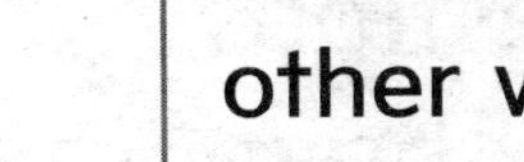

I like my barrio because

Find Text Evidence

Ask questions you may have before reading the story. Then read to find the answers.

Circle the word **Do**.

Sid

Do Sid and Mom like it?

Shared Read

Find Text Evidence

Circle an object on page 40 whose name begins with the same sound as **dip**.

Underline words that tell what Dan can do.

Sid and Mom do like it!

Dan can tap, tap on a door.

Shared Read

Find Text Evidence

Circle the picture of Dot on page 42.

Underline words on page 43 that begin with the same sound as **did**.

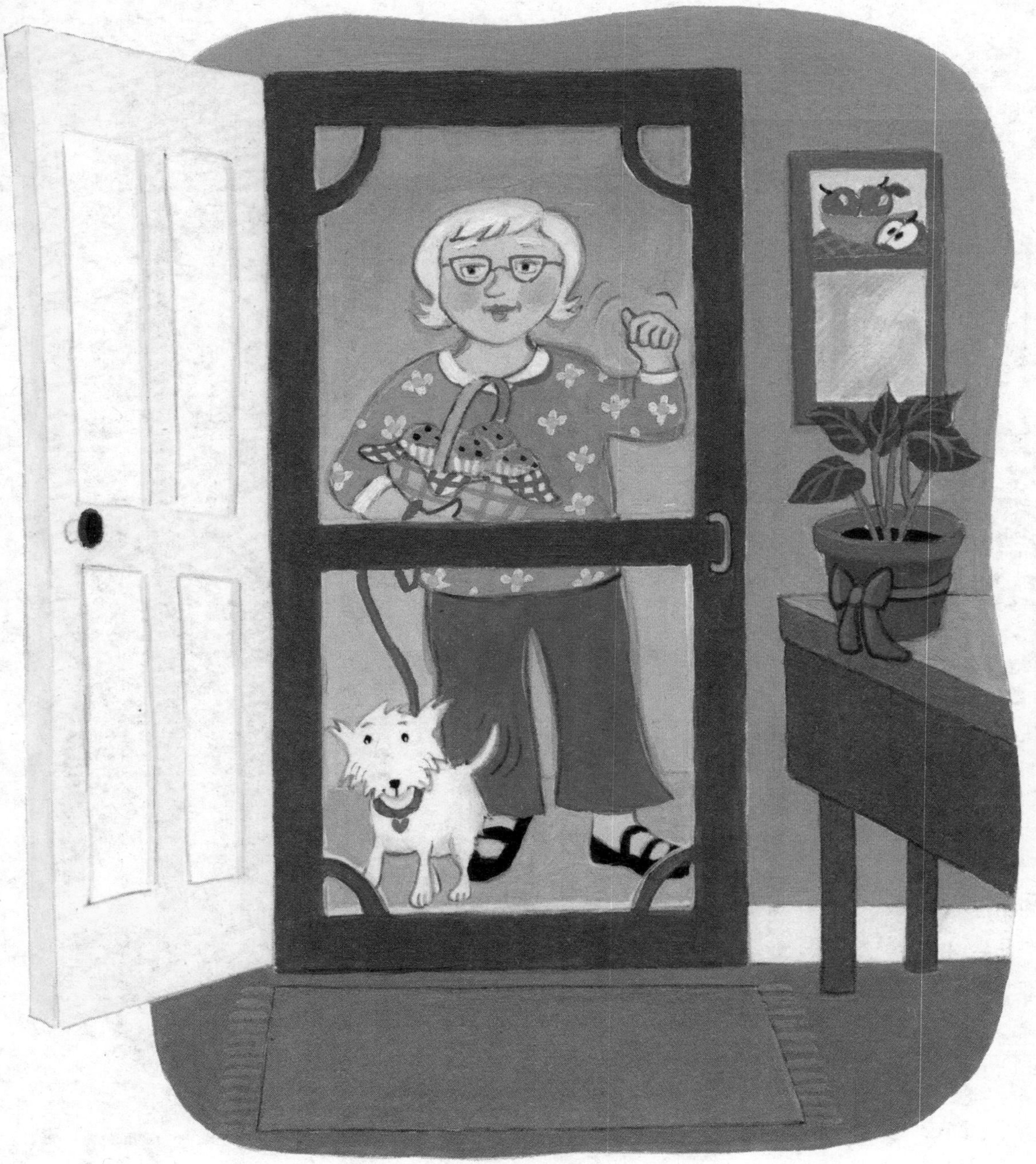

Dot can tap, tap on a door.

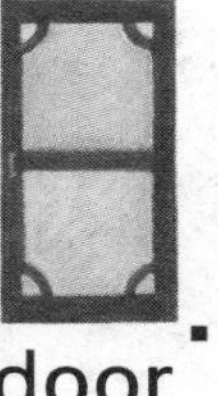

Dot and Dan can sip.

Shared Read

Find Text Evidence

Circle words that end with the same sound as **sad**.

Retell the story. Use the words and pictures to help you.

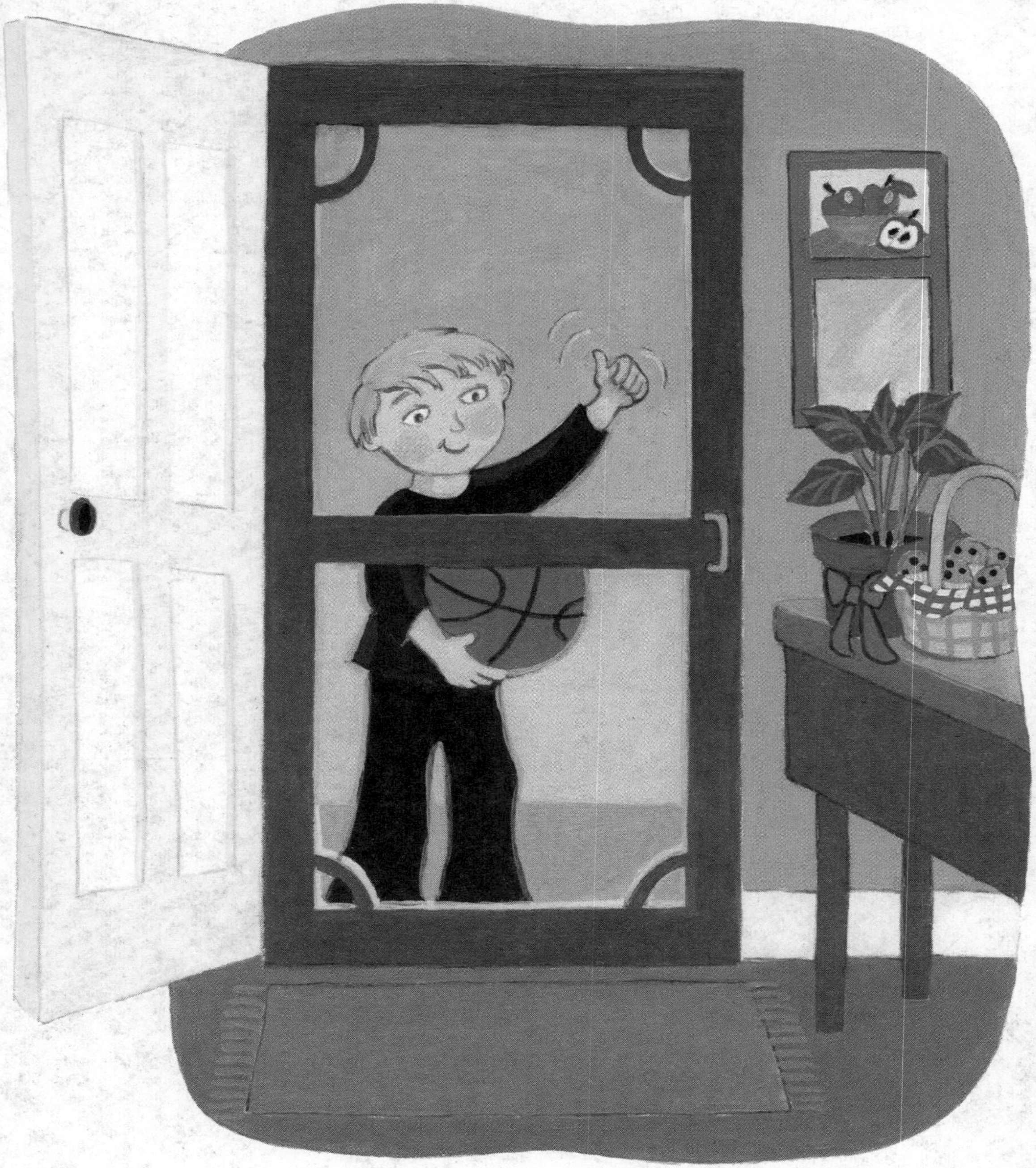

Tod can tap, tap on a .

Sid and Tod pat a ball.

Listen to page 33.

Quick Tip

Caleb wrote this story about his neighborhood. He used words such as *I* and *my*. This kind of story is called a **personal narrative**.

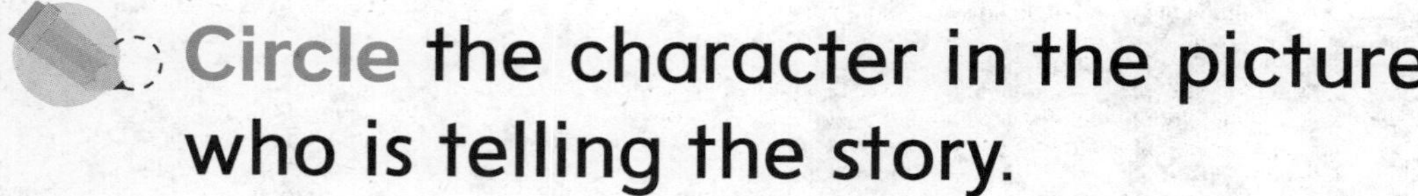

Circle the character in the picture who is telling the story.

Write his name. Tell what he likes to do.

Talk about the places where Caleb goes in his neighborhood.

Draw a place where Caleb goes. Show what he does there.

Write About It

Caleb wrote a personal narrative about himself and what he likes to do. Now write about yourself and what you like to do.

What Neighbors Do

Step 1 **Talk** about different things neighbors do together.

Step 2 **Write** a question about things neighbors do together.

Step 3 **Ask** classmates and neighbors your question.

Step 4 **Draw** what you learned.

Step 5 **Choose** a good way to present your work.

Make Connections

Talk about what these neighbors are doing together. How are they having fun?

Compare these neighbors to the neighbors in *What Can You Do with a Paleta?*

Quick Tip

We can look for **clues**, or details, in photos to help us answer questions.

What I Know Now

Think about the texts you read this week.

The texts tell about

Think about what you learned this week.
What else would you like to learn?
Talk about your ideas.

Share one thing you learned about
realistic fiction stories.

Talk About It

Essential Question **How can people help to make their community better?**

Talk about how these children pitch in to make their neighborhood better.

Draw and **write** about how you can pitch in to help your neighborhood.

We can help our neighborhood by

Jade Albert Studio, Inc./The Image Bank/Getty Images

Respond to the Big Book

 **Retell** the nonfiction text.

 **Write** about the text.

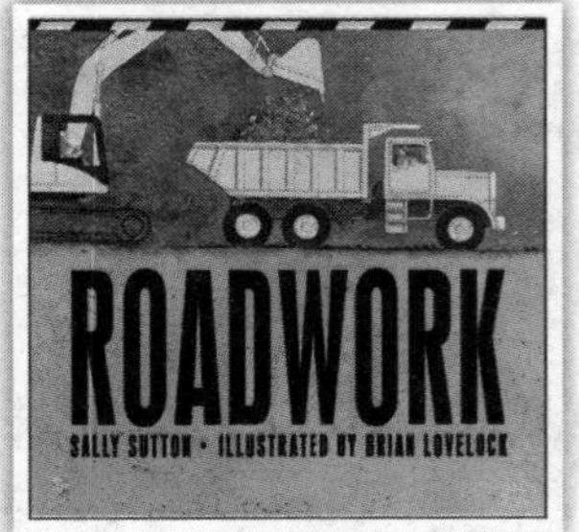

An interesting fact I learned is

Text Evidence
Page

I know this text is nonfiction because

Text Evidence
Page

Talk about workers who help your community.

Draw a worker who helps.

Share how the worker you drew helps your community.

Combine Information

Many workers are needed to build a road. How does each worker add something important?

Reread **Big Book**

An author tells the events in a certain order, or sequence. Words such as <u>first</u>, <u>next</u>, and <u>last</u> tell the sequence.

 **Listen** to part of the text.

 **Talk** about what happens **first, next,** and **last**.

 **Draw** what happens.

First

Next

Last

Reread **Big Book**

Listen to pages 14–15.
What words does the author use to tell about the sounds?

Talk about how these words help you know what the workers are doing.

Write your ideas.

The words help me know

Listen to page 32. Why do you think the author added this page?

Talk about the different machines and their facts.

Draw one of the machines. Show a fact about it.

I Can, You Can!

Ask questions about the story before you read. This can help you understand the story. Then read to find out what the mom and girl can do.

Circle the words **and, go,** and **to.**

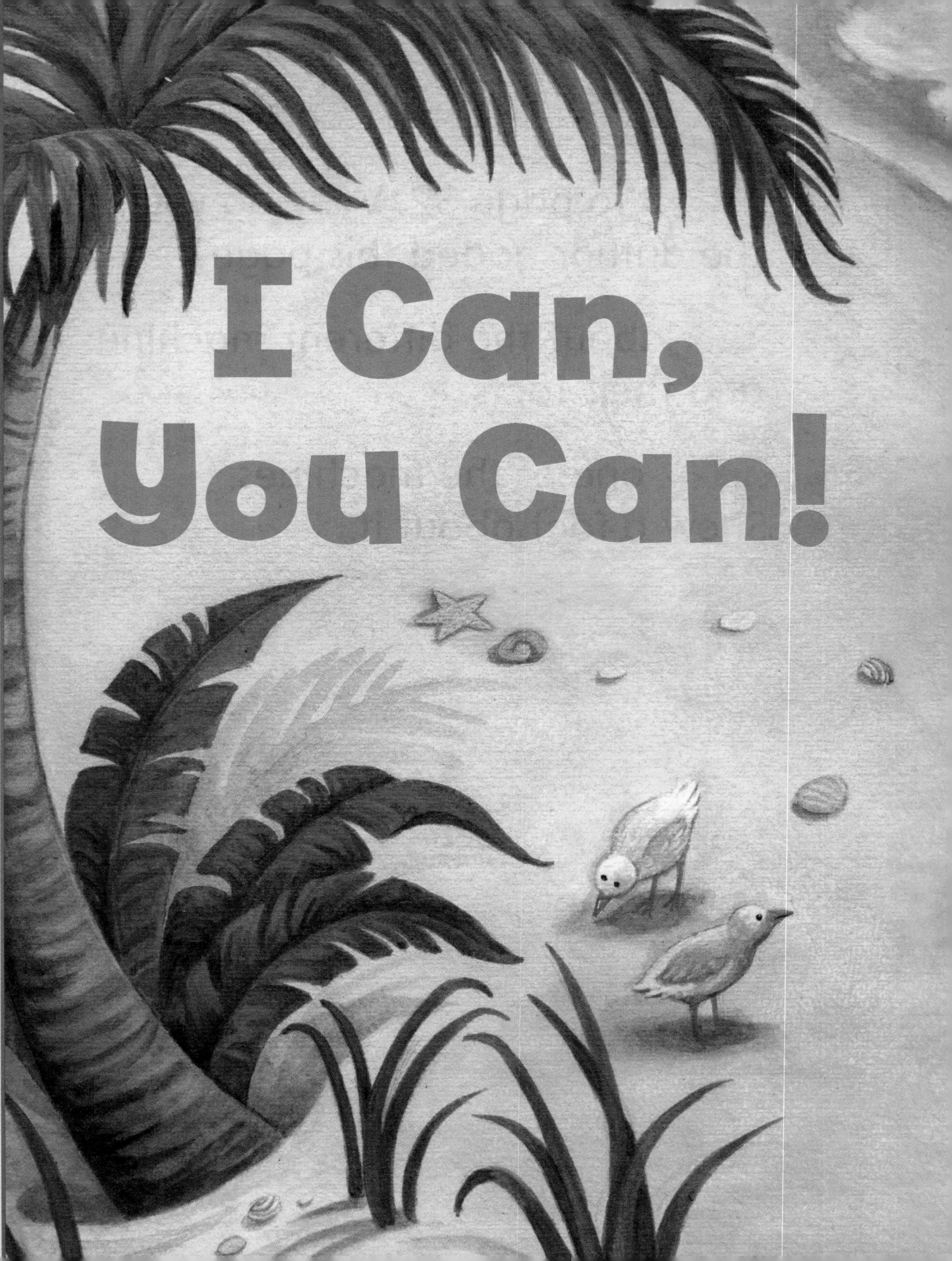

Mom and I go to a  .
beach

Shared Read

Find Text Evidence

Circle what the girl can pat, pat, pat.

Underline the word **you**.

I can pat, pat, pat on top.

Can you pat it?

Shared Read

Find Text Evidence

Circle the picture of **Stan**.

Underline the word that begins with the same sounds as **spin**.

I can tip, tip it on top.

Stan can spot it.

Shared Read

Find Text Evidence

Circle the word that begins with the same sounds as **snip**.

Retell the story. Use the words and pictures to help you.

I can pat, pat, pat on top.

We can do it in a snap!

Paired Selection

Look at the photos. How can people work together to plant a garden?

First they dig. Next they plant seeds. Then they water.

Talk about the words that help you know the order of each step.

Circle the words that tell the order.

Talk about what happens when the vegetables are ready to pick.

Write what happens last.

Last

Talk About It

Talk about ways people can help to make a garden. How can a garden help a community?

Making Our School Better

Step 1 **Talk** about ways you can make your school community better.

Step 2 **Write** a question about things you can do to help your school.

Step 3 **Ask** classmates and school workers your question.

Step 4 **Draw** and **write** about what you learned.

We can make our school better by

____

____

Step 5 **Choose** a good way to present your work.

Integrate

Make Connections

Talk about how these people pitch in to help their community.

Compare how these people help their community to how the workers in *Roadwork* help their community.

Quick Tip

To talk about helping, we can use these words:

donate, pitch in, volunteer

These people donate clothing and other items to people who need them.

JUPITERIMAGES/Brand X/Alamy

What I Know Now

Think about the texts you read this week.

The texts tell about

Think about what you learned this week. What else would you like to learn? Talk about your ideas.

Share one thing you learned about nonfiction texts.

Writing and Grammar

I wrote a personal narrative. It is a story that tells about something that happened to me.

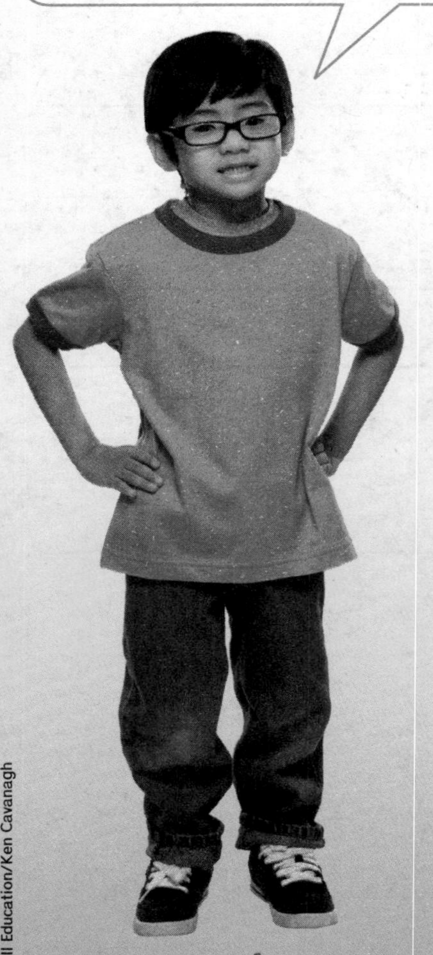

McGraw-Hill Education/Ken Cavanagh

Personal Narrative
My personal narrative tells about an event that was special to me.

Student Model

My Mystery Trip

My Uncle Shiro took me to the airport.
But we did not get on a plane.
We watched gigantic jets land and take off.
It was loud.
I had so much fun!

Genre Study

Talk about what makes Yoshi's writing a personal narrative.

Ask any questions you have about personal narratives.

Circle how Yoshi feels about the trip.

Writing and Grammar

Plan

Talk about something that happened to you.

Draw what happened.

Quick Tip

Think of an event that was special to you.

Write what your personal narrative is about.

My personal narrative is about

Draw a detail that happened.

Draft

Read Yoshi's draft of his personal narrative.

Quick Tip

Remember: A **draft** is the first writing we do.

We write and organize our ideas.

Student Model

A Trip to the Airport

My Uncle Shiro took me to the airport.
But we did not get on a plane.
We watched jets.
I had so much fun!

Sequence
I put the events in order.

I included a detail that tells more about what happened.

Your Turn

Begin to write your personal narrative in your writer's notebook. Use your ideas from pages 76–77.

Writing and Grammar

Revise and Edit

Think about how Yoshi revised and edited his personal narrative.

I made sure to spell the high-frequency word *the* correctly.

Student Model

I wrote a better title.

My Mystery Trip

My Uncle Shiro took me to the airport.
But we did not get on a plane.
We watched gigantic jets land and take off.
It was loud.
I had so much fun!

I added a **sentence**. It tells a complete idea.

I added an **adjective**.

I added details to make my writing more interesting.

Grammar

- A **sentence** is a group of words that tells a complete idea.
- An **adjective,** or describing word, tells more about a noun.

I added more details to my picture.

Your Turn

Revise and edit your personal narrative. Be sure to use complete sentences and adjectives. Use your checklist.

Share and Evaluate

Practice presenting your work with a partner. Take turns.

Present your work. Then use this checklist.

Sharing My Work	Yes	No
Writing and Grammar		
I wrote a personal narrative.	☐	☐
I put the events in order.	☐	☐
I added details.	☐	☐
I used complete sentences.	☐	☐
I used adjectives.	☐	☐
Speaking and Listening		
I spoke in a loud, clear voice.	☐	☐
I listened carefully.	☐	☐
I asked questions.	☐	☐

Talk with a partner about your writing.

Write about your work.

What did you do well in your writing?

What do you need to work on?

Show What You Learned

Spiral Review

Genre
- Fable
- Nursery Rhyme
- Nonfiction

Skill
- Character, Setting, Events
- Rhyme and Rhythm
- Sequence

Focus on Fables

A fable is a made-up story from long ago. A fable teaches a lesson.

 Listen to "The Bundle of Sticks." Think about what makes this story a fable.

 Talk and write about the main characters and the setting.

The main characters are

The setting is

Draw an important event.

Talk about the lesson that this fable teaches.

Show What You Learned

Focus on Nonfiction

The events in a nonfiction text are often told in a certain order, or sequence.

Listen to part of "Lady Bird Cleans Up."

Talk about what Lady Bird did **first**, **next**, and **last**.

Draw what happened.

First

Kagenmi/iStock/Getty Images

Next

Last

Extend Your Learning

Choose Your Own Book

Quick Tip

Try to read a little longer each time you read.

Write the title of the book.

Tell a partner why you want to read it. Then read the book.

Minutes I Read

Write your opinion of the book.

What Did You Learn?

Think about the skills you have learned.
How do you feel about what you can do?

Circle a picture in each row.

I understand character, setting, and events.			
I understand rhyme and rhythm.			
I understand sequence.			

Talk with a partner about something you want to get better at.

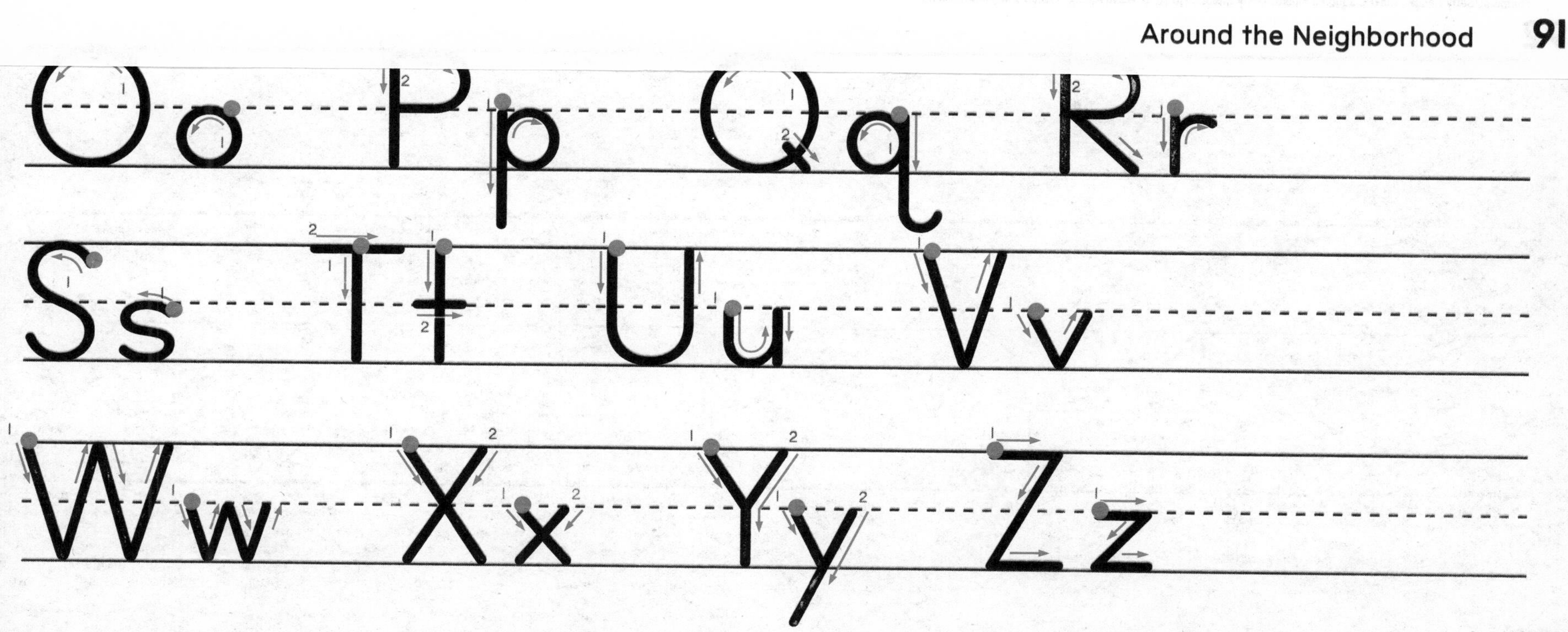

My Sound-Spellings

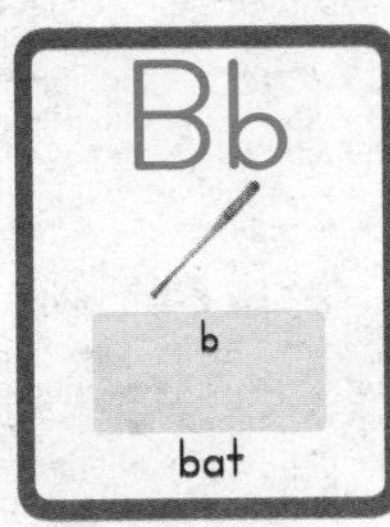

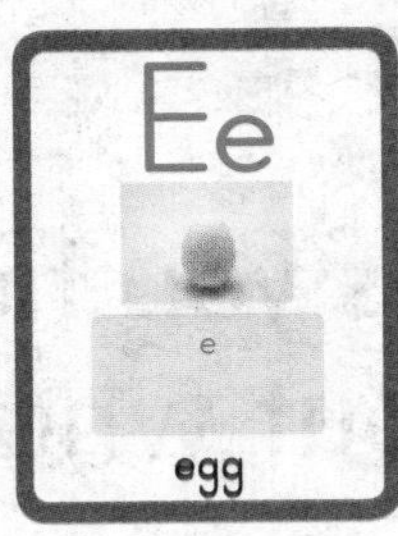